J. Delg

THE EVIL BANALITY OF RACISM: PUERTO RICO AND CUBA BEFORE AND AFTER TAPIA Y RIVERA'S *THE QUADROON*

United States • Bogotá • Sydney

Ediciones El Laberinto
Calle 9 Núm. 26-46
Bogotá 111971, Colombia
+57 489 7989

U.S.A. Distributor: amazon.com

Cover Design: Paolo A. Tous
Interior Design: Mizraím Orlani

Composición deTalleres El Laberinto
Bogotá, Colombia

Contents

Note for the Reader

I am well aware that contemporary scholarship prefers the formats prescribed by the American Psychological Association (APA) for notes and references. I have s strong dislike of endnotes that require the reader to go in search of references, then having to return to the page to continue reading. Therefore, I have chosen to use footnotes, with apologies to the appropriate authorities.

THE EVIL BANALITY OF RACISM: PUERTO RICO AND CUBA BEFORE AND AFTER TAPIA Y RIVERA'S *THE QUADROON*

The Drama's Plot

Julia is the quadroon, *cuarterona*, the daughter of a white man and a black slave. The term *quadroon* refers to a person who is one-fourth of African origin. The Countess has raised her as a chamber maid under her protection, for which Julia is grateful and feels a deep obligation to obey her mistress

7

for the latter's charitable assistance. The Countess is a widowed aristocratic land-owner in Havana toward the mid-nineteenth century. Her son Carlos is in love with Julia, but racial and class prejudice make it impossible for them to pursue a romantic relationship. Julia is conflicted in her own love for the Countess's son, due to her duty to obey and honor her mistress, who, at learning of Carlos' intentions toward Julia becomes intensely opposed to the relationship. The mother's motives are actually twofold: to keep Carlos and Julia away from each other with lies about Julia's possible origins (the Countess claims, knowing it to be false), that Julia may be Carlos' father's illegitimate daughter), and to facilitate a marriage between Emilia and her son. Emilia is the daughter of Don Críspulo, a wealthy social climber involved in the illicit slave trade who will save the Countess from financial ruin and a subsequent loss of prestige, while Don Críspulo will obtain a nobility title through marriage. The Countess forces Carlos into marrying Emilia; while the ceremony is taking place, Julia becomes aware of it and makes a fatal decision regarding her life.

The Nature of Racism

Any discussion about racism in *La cuarterona* must necessarily begin by considering the presence of Africans in the Americas, the nature of racism and the social context that frames the drama.

For the purposes of this exploration racism is an attempt at control by the class perceived as hegemonic through the stratification of ethnicity and the intensity of melanin. When the attempt succeeds, the conviction of superiority is set, depriving the perceived inferior class of will, value and freedom. This

dispossession becomes evident with the obligation to produce for the superior class without the offer by the class or expectation of the inferior of any compensation. In this sense racism is an *ipso facto* form of constructive slavery, although racism itself is a prerequisite of the institution of slavery.

One way of expressing the power of the master over the slave is to violate the right to sexual intimacy as physically as possible. Violent penetration is a sublimation of a stabbing that does not kill, an irrelevant consideration, because it is, symbolically, equivalent to murder. Ironically, this act can lead to the propagation of the rapist's racial lineage in the embodiment of a social pariah.[1]

---

[1] In Don Crispín's case, in *La cuarterona* the horror of the rape is only evinced when the quadroon dies and the catalyst character of Jorge reveals that the dead woman was, first, the fruit of abuse through the slave ownberj's implicit right and, second, because everyone has learned the secret, including his legitimate daughter, who then knows the real man. The sexual object is

The agent that precipitates the racist tendency in the Americas is, therefore, African slavery. Racism and prejudice in both the northern and the southern continents in the western hemisphere have led to insidious forms of inequality and exclusion against indigenous peoples since the first landing of Columbus on that side of the world and up to our days, The blending of native populations with Europeans, *el mestizaje indígena*, is beyond the scope of this analysis, whose focus is racism against African slaves and their descendants in the Caribbean and, more precisely, Cuba and Puerto Rico. The starting point for this study is the dramatic representation of racism and its consequences as presented in Alejandro Tapia y Rivera's play *La cuarterona, The Quadroon*.

---

of no importance, but keeping appearances to pass for a moral person is of vital importance.

Six centuries of Shackles, Branding and Stigma

The slave trade was officially conducted in Spanish American colonies from 1513 to 1820. The first slaves were brought to Cuba in 1517 under the authorization of emperor Charles I of Spain, with the purpose of adding cheap labor in the Spanish colonies. (In Spanish the reference to manual labor is *mano de obra*, a synecdoche, "hand for work, interesting to the extent that only the hands of slaves were given any value aside from sexual organs.) In 1817 Bourbon king Ferdinand VII decreed the prohibition of importation of new slaves into Spanish territories by 1820. Smuggling did not end until much later, toward the end of the nineteenth century.

La cuarterona's author was the Puerto Rican playwright Alejandro Tapia y Rivera. He wrote the play in Havana and Madrid, where he honed the text and shared it with others who likewise participated in his abolitionist philosophy. Tapia y Rivera published the play in 1867 and opened in San Juan in 1878.

The play is set in Havana, where the situation of slaves was similar to that of Tapia y Rivera's native Puerto Rico. Therefore, the analysis of both locations is relevant, considering that the author knew both places well, and both Cuba and Puerto Rico shared historical colonial profiles in most significant aspects.

According to censuses at the time, 1,892 people inhabited Puerto Rico in 1531. Of these 369 were white and 1,523 were slaves. Toward mid-nineteenth century the population had risen to 583,181, of which 300,430 were white Europeans. The rest were 41,736 slaves and free blacks and biracial persons. In Cuba by mid-nineteenth century 400,000 slaves.[2]

---

[2] The historical background of slavery in Puerto Rico and other Caribbean territories is presented in: Francisco A. Scarano, *Puerto Rico, cinco siglos de historia* (México: McGraw-Hill Interamericana, 2006), Stephen Palmié and Francisco A. Scarano (eds.), *The Caribbean: A History of Its Region and Its People* (Chicago: The University of Chicago Press, 2011), Luis A. Figueroa, *Sugar, Slavery, and Freedom*

The social structure in the Spanish American colonies between the eighteenth and nineteenth centuries ranked, from highest to lowest in terms of influence and power, first, viceroys, governors, the military; the latter was also in charge of public order); the landowning oligarchy, descendants of he original colonizers; the clergy of the Catholic church, the only religious institution officially allowed and to which membership was obligatory; peninsular entrepreneurs.

Social classes under the dominance of the ruling strata were *criollos*, white natives that represented a fledgling bourgeoisie; poor whites; freed slaves; *encomendado* (parceled) indigenous tribes under the control of Catholic missionary priests and of whom few had survived past sixteenth century; African slaves..[3]

---

in *Nineteenth Century Puerto Rico* (Chapel Hill: The University of North Carolina Press, 2005).

[3] See Yankiel Pérez, "Cuba colonial, 1492-1898", *Contribuciones a las Ciencias Sociales* (Universidad de Málaga), Octubre 2010; Javier Figueroa Ledón, "El negro y la integración racial durante la primera década republicana",

Suspicion and prejudice against African slaves in colonial society originated in fear that can be summarized as follows: (1) Racial war, the dread of which was fed by the slave revolution in Haiti in 1791. (2) African religious practices, seen as competing with Catholic Christian beliefs. (3) Black sexuality. Black men were seen as rapists of white women; women of mixed race were seen as seducers, lascivious and untrustworthy.[4]

In 1812 the Spanish "Constitution of Cádiz" granted Spanish citizenship to Puerto Ricans, but excluded slaves.

In 1834 England ended slavery, including the island of Jamaica. Spain and Brazil remained the only countries in the western hemisphere that did not proscribe slavery. In 1843 Spain entered into an agreement with other European nations to pursue and prosecute slave smugglers

---

Contribuciones a las Ciencias Sociales (Universidad de Málaga), Diciembre 2010.

[4] See Sujatha Fernandez, "Fear of a Black Nation: Local Rappers and Crossings and State Power in Contemporary Cuba," *Anthropological Quarterly* 76:4, 2003, pp. 575-608.

from Africa. The treaty, however, had no effect in reducing the slave trade.

Since the mid-eighteenth century and until the period ended Cuba experienced the threat of a slave revolt. Whites began to feel the terror of being annihilated by the slaves' superior strength and numbers. With the Haitian rebellion in 1797 the fear intensified, particularly because Haiti's rebels not only destroyed sugar cane fields (thereby propitiating a significant increase in sugar production in Cuba), but also murdered white colonizers and their families.

In 1806 Cuba forbade marriage between people of differing races, in an attempt to prevent the growth of a hybrid race that would undermine white influence and power. Ferdinand VII's Royal Order of December 21, 1817 promoted the migration of Catholic Europeans to Cuba. Newly arrived colonizers were exempted from tithing and allowed to carry firearms.

As in all societies that operate on the basis of racial distinction and attributes to "the other," "what is different," and specially if "the other" has distinctive physical features and linguistic traits, every calamitous ill, black Africans were considered the worst elements of society among the dominant classes. All moral failings of Cuban society came from the black population, specifically the *mulato*: prostitution, criminality in general, superstition, lust and laziness.[5]

Enormous irony derives from the fact that the greatest and most revered hero of the Cuban war for independence from Spain was General José Antonio de la Caridad Maceo y Grajales. Maceo was of mixed races. He is known as "The Bronze Titan." Likewise, General Fulgencio Batista, who was first elected and then usurped power to become dictator from 1952 until 1958, with the acquiescence and support of the American government and corporations, was also of blended races. (The 1990 film

---

[5] Aline Helg, *Our Rightful Share: The Afro-Cuban Struggle for Equality, 1886-1915* (Chapel Hill, North Carolina: The University of North Carolina Press, 1995), pp. 25 and ff; Alejandro de la Fuente, *A Nation for All: Envisioning* Cuba (Chapel Hill: The University of North Carolina Press, 2001), pp. 30 and ff.

Havana erroneously presented him as white.)

No slave rebellions were attempted in Puerto Rico as the ones in Cuba, Martinique and St. Croix early in the nineteenth century. Early in 1843 small uprisings took place in Toa Baja, Ponce and other communities. Five years later the colonial governor, Field Marshall Juan Prim enforced what was known as the "Negro Code." It authorized slave masters to punish slaves physically. It also exacted the death penalty for any rebellions. The proactive measures were meant to forestall any initiative similar to the ones in neighboring islands, where Prim had sent military reinforcements to aid French and Danish colonial administrations. The decree mandated military processes without any intervention from civil authorities against Africans who committed crimes against the white population. The code was enforced during six months.

Toward the mid-nineteenth century liberals and reformers in Puerto Rico had begun efforts to obtain the abolition of slavery. The abolitionists were headed by Ramón Emeterio Betances, Segundo Ruiz Belvis, Julio Vizcarrondo and José Julián Acosta, first in the island and later in Spain. As a reformer, Betances wrote "The Ten Commandments of Free Men:" freedom of religion, speech, the press, commerce, assembly, as well as the right to bear arms, the inviolability of a citizen and the right of the governed to elect its own government. The document further emphasized he abolition of slavery.

In the Spanish city of Cádiz in 1868 José Julián Acosta presented in the Spanish Courts a project for the abolition of slavery that was strenuously opposed by powerful business and local government interests. The opposition did not deter the abolitionist movement. Eventually the reformers were supported by King Amadeo I of Savoy. Shortly after establishing the First Republic of Spain, the king signed the "Law of the Abolition of Slavery in Puerto Rico" on March 22, 1873. The law provided for the indemnification to former slave owners. It also required that the latter contract former slaves during a three-year period of paid labor. Five years later slaves would be entitled to all the rights of free citizens. Abolition, however, would end neither racism nor its psychological or social consequences of slavery.

In both Puerto Rico and Cuba segments of the mixed-race population that reject their African origins. Five centuries of humiliation and identification as inferior and unworthy have left deep scars in the psyche of black people and their blended-race descendants. The concept of self among such segments of the population of descendants of the former slaves has been shaped mediated by the white population's vision of black behavior, leading black people to censure themselves and others of their race and to judge themselves against the same standard set by the old master. In Cuba a drop of white blood is enough for a person to claim racial whiteness. In addition, there is an unofficial effort, a tacit conspiracy by the government to whiten (*blanquear*) Cuban society, despite government assertions that Cuba is a completely integrated and egalitarian society. To denounce any kind of racial inequality in Cuba is a crime punishable by imprisonment. (It mirrors the USSR under Stalin, when murder was not recognized as an act only possible in capitalist societies, not in the Marxist Leninist paradise: murders were always attributed to wild-animal attacks or accidents.) However, the Central Committee of the Cuban Communist Party's membership for decades was all white: the only black member was the world-known poet Nicolás Guillén, who was already a member of the Communist Party in the early 50s (which earned him the refusal of a tourist visa to the U.S.) and whose antipathy toward the United States, particularly when compared to the benevolent Soviet Union, was evident in his poetry. The Cuban population census of 1980, which depends on individual declarations regarding self-perceived race, states that Cuba was 60% black. In the 2002 census the white population was 65%; this would have required a remarkable and very unlikely influx of white people or an inordinate birth rate among the white population.[6] International demographic organizations have categorized Cuban censuses as unreliable.

It is particularly curious that Cuban post-revolution exiles have transported their racism to their enclaves in southern Florida, New Jersey, New York and elsewhere. Not a single member of professional Cuban elites or vested with financial or political influence in the United States is even of mixed races. Among these are: congresswoman Ileana Ros-Lehtiner, senators Marco Rubio, Eduardo Cruz and Bob Menéndez; Cuban actors Andy Garcia, William Levy and Steven Bauer; TV personality and entrepreneur Cristina Saralegui; entrepreneurs Raúl Alarcón, Jr. and Jorge Mas Canosa (communications mogul, founder of

[6] "Heroic Myth and Prosaic Failure", *The Economist*, December 2008, www.theeconomist.com/node/12851254. "Obama Effect Highlights Racism in Cuba", *New American Media*, Dec. 15, 2008.

the fiercely anti-Castro reactionary Cuban American National Foundation and whose net worth at his death was calculated in over $100 million); the Bacardi heirs and the Diaz-Balart brothers (José, Rafael and Lincoln, whose cousin is Fidel Castro's son); Miami mayor Xavier Suárez; developer Jorge Pérez. Naturally, those Cubans, natives or first-generation U.S. citizens, arrived on American soil with professional diplomas, connections and anxious to make a go of their life in the U.S., a country they only knew from vacations in the mainland, former jobs with or consumption of products of American-based corporations in Cuba or through American tourists and American popular culture. Those who came as exiles initially impoverished and ignorant of English had the advantage of their skin color (except in Puerto Rico, where many moved to be on U.S. soil and still able to speak Spanish: Puerto Ricans almost universally hated them). The racial configuration allowed them a less difficult access to American society, particularly in the racist South and despite rampant xenophobia in Florida.

Toward the end of the 70s the Cuban presence in the spheres of power was noticeable, although even Cubans with professional titles had to take jobs as janitors and vegetable pickers in Florida. These began extending networks within organizations that allowed them horizontal and vertical mobility. The employment dynamic had a negative impact on the black population of Florida. Traditionally the lower-paying jobs that Cubans were then taking, for lower wages than blacks had been able to obtain and for longer hours, had been open primarily to poor uneducated blacks. While white xenophobes in Florida resented the influx of Cuban exiles early in the 60s, the displacement of the black population from neighborhoods generally perceived as humble black districts resulted in open hostility between Cubans and blacks. Anyone visiting a metropolitan area in Florida immediately notices the distance between the two groups.

The situation has worsened in the twenty-first century with the increase of Puerto Ricans due to hurricanes or economic hardship, who carry with them the germ of resentment and antipathy toward Cubans and the *gringo*—and worse if it is a black *gringo*.

In the early 60s Puerto Ricans resented employment competition in the private sector from eager Cubans forced to make an impression with their hard work just to survive. In a perverse way white Cubans became the equivalent of blacks for racists. The mere mention of a Cuban needed no explanation: it was an implicit negative remark. Often Cubans were referred to with a distinctively dismissive position of an adjective. In Spanish tne postposition of an adjective often changes the meaning of the phrase: *ese coche* (that car) indicates a specific car; *el carro* ése is the equivalent of that damned car. In Puerto Rico it was much more common to hear *el cubano ése* than *ese cubano*. In the neighborhood where I grew up parents warned their children to stay away from the Cubans down the street. Cuban students were looked down upon at private schools, while many Cubans attended such institutions instead of public schools. Puerto Rican students would call them *expatriados*, which normally would mean just expatriates, but in that context it was closer to "people without a country," pariahs.

In the Miami Dade area protests by public servants such as bus drivers against the requirement that they speak Spanish were useless. By the early 70s businesses actively recruited bilingual employees to deal with non-English speaking Cubans. The first wave of exiles harbored the hope of returning to Cuba once Castro was removed from power. Given the temporary nature of their stay in the U.S., they had no need to speak the new language. As time passed and it became obvious that a return was unlikely, they still refused to learn English unless it was necessary to attain employment. Their children, however, were more practical and were forced into speaking English by the educational system. Today the presence of Cuban eiles and their descendants in most metropolitan areas of Florida, as well as in various regions in the northern states and California, is undeniable in businesses, not only because Cubans work there, but because often they also own them). Since the late twentieth century that presence has blended with Latinos of every possible nationality, particularly in Florida. In Puerto Rico Cubans have even held elected positions in local government.

Equally interesting is the fact that a flourishing and significant population of Chinese nationals and descendants lived in Havana in the *Barrio Chino*, Chinatown. They had been there since the mid-nineteenth century, as they had come to other regions in the Americas to work in railroad construction and the laundry industry. They were aware of Mao Tse-Tung's China and were not about to live under communist rule. Many fled when the Revolution expropriated and nationalized their businesses. Little, if anything, is known of them in exile.

Today Cuban youth in the island quietly complain about the low place of people of African origins hold in state-run institutions and their absence in the leadership of labor unions. Otherwise, they realize that the destiny of Cuba is in the hands of what they call a "white gerontocracy."

In the 60s black Cubans were discouraged from attempting to leave their country with stories of American racism (not exactly misleading). Around that time a joke went around about a black Cuban couple in Miami who go past a building sign that reads: "Furnished Apartment for Rent." The man says to his wife: "Look at this! The government in Cuba says they don't want blacks here, but look at this sign: apartment rented *niche*." *Niche* is the pejorative term for blacks in Cuba, derived from the English *nigger*.

In terms of gender and race, Puerto Rico is full of contradictions, despite the incidence of both racism and misogyny.

The first speaker of the island's House of Representatives was Erneso Ramos Antonini, a black lawyer who paid for his law-school tuition by playing the piano in local clubs in San Juan. The most prominent leader of Puerto Rican nationalism, a Harvard law graduate, Pedro Albizu Campos, was also of black roots.

Then again, at a different level, racism is prevalent among the higher classes in Puerto Rico. In the middle and lower class it is not unusual to find people who express racist remarks despite the presence of an African ancestry in their lives. The Puerto Rican poet Fortunato Vizcarrondo (1899-1977) epitomized the attitude in his "Y tu abuela, ¿dónde está?" The prolonged apostrophe addresses someone who makes fun up dark people and their features, then asks: "And your grandma, where is she?" to allude to the habit among some Puerto Ricans of purposely hiding any trace of an African genealogy. In thiss case the grandmother is hidden in the kitchen.

In the town where I grew up in south-eastern Puerto Rico, there was a man with white features was known to be an unrepentant racist who constantly dug into other people's past to identify their ancestral blackness. I met his grandmother when she was in her deathbed around the early 60s. I was surprised to realize she was one of the darkest-skinned people I had ever seen. Her son's reddish hair was tightly curled. The racist's daughter's facial features betrayed an obvious African background. It never deterred him from his racist remarks.

In the late 1960s a group of students at the exclusive boarding school I attended in Puerto Rico, *Colegio San Antonio Abad,* initiateded what they called a chapter of the Ku Klux Klan. The group was brazenly racist against non-white students; the Minnesotan priests who ran the school were indifferent to the phenomenon and were even tacitly encouraging with their own prejudice even against other black monks in their monastic community. It never crossed the racist group's mind that being Catholic and Puerto Rican would have excluded them from membership in the actual organization and instead make them targets of their violence.

When I was a senior n that same school we had a classmate, a transfer student who came from a prestigious Jesuit school in the San Juan metropolitan area, *Colegio San Ignacio*. When I asked him whether he knew another student in the same school he replied with a question: "Isn't he a nigger?" The young man to whom he referred was my godmother's son; yes, his curls were tight and his skin was darker than most whites', most likely due to his father's side of the family. I have never forgiven myself for not asking him what that had to do with anything and instead remained silent. Both the racist and the object of his prejudice are prominent Puerto Rican surgeons.

On the female inequality side, economic and social pressures have driven women to the job market, in contrast with the traditional view of women as homemakers and wives. Until the late 50s that was the rule: only women of the lower classes and those who dared defy the macho-centric perspective because of attainment of higher education degrees went to work outside their homes. Women in the middle class and higher were expected to quit working, if they did so, and stay home cleaning house and looking after the children, often with the help of a live-in maid or cook or a maid who cooked. However, unless assisted by a servant, to this day working women are generally expected to come home to cook, do laundry and clean before helping children with homework, bathing them and putting them to bed.

Nonetheless, in terms of female participation in public life in Puerto Rico since the 40s, local political leadership included women. The first mayor of a capital city in the Americas was Felisa Rincón de Gautier, mayor of San Juan (1946-1968). María Luisa Arcelay was a progressive leader and businesswoman who was elected to the Puerto Rico House of Representatives in 1932. Puerto Rico has had a female governor in the twentieth century; in 2012 her daughter was also elected to the Puerto Rican legislature. Jennifer Gonzalez was elected resident commissioner for Puerto Rico in the U.S. House of Representatives in 2016.

The rights of women in the area of pay equality was set in Puerto Rico in 1948, at least in public service. Wages are determined by a fixed scale that only takes into account the person's education and experience to determine appointments and promotions. Factors such as race, gender or social origin do not enter into consideration. In the state of Georgia as recently as 2019, the mayor of the town of Hoschton, fifty miles north of the state capital of Atlanta, declared that her administration would not hire African Americans, because her city was not ready to hire such people.

Governors in Puerto Rico were appointed by the president of the U.S. from 1898 to 1948. The first governor of Puerto Rican origin was Jesús T. Piñero; Luis

Muñoz Marín, previously president of the island's legislature's senate, was elected by Puerto Ricans the same year that Piñero's governorship came to an end after the U.S. federal government granted Puerto Ricans the right to vote for their own governor. As soon as the Spanish American war ended in 1898, a military governor was appointed in Puerto Rico, starting with General Nelson Miles. Eventually Charles Herbert Allen, a civil governor (1900), was granted the post. Appointees by the U.S. to occupy the governorship of Puerto Rico were white. Since Puerto Ricans started electing their governor, no one has been kept from running for office for reasons of gender or race.

Nonetheless, what might be called Puerto *Ricanhood* includes two outstanding features, although they are not unique to Puerto Ricans and aside from all the positive characteristics of the Puerto Rican people, but equally undeniable: racism and homophobia (or more accurately, homomisia, hatred of homosexuals rather than fear of them).

Puerto Rican nonverbal communication and spoken expressions reveal a generalized prejudice.[7] In what is generally called "polite company," Puerto Ricans run their index finger up and down a forearm to indicate that a person is either black or a descendant of Africans even when their features are not necessarily black. In a concealed fashion they make small circles with a finger on their hair to point out to someone's suspiciously curly hair. Behind a person's back Puerto Ricans will extend an arm out and make their wrist limp to indicate someone is homosexual. One of the quickest ways to lose favor in a political campaign or be voted out is to be called *pato* or *pata* (literally, gander or duck; metaphorically a fag or a dyke). Doubtlessly the argument can be made that it is

---

[7] The communication of the unpleasant through signs in Puerto Rico is detailed in Carmen Judith Nine-Curt, *Non-Verbal Communication in Puerto Rico* (Cambridge, MA: Evaluation, Dissemination and Assessment Center for Bilingual Eduation, 1984).

the same in all Spanish American countries; Spain has long ago begun to relieve the stigma attached to homosexuality as a hindrance to occupying elected office, and allows same-sex families to live in public-service communities such as compounds for law-enforcement officers.

"He's a black man with a white soul" is a common racist expression in Puerto Rico. So is: "The black man, if he doesn't do something nasty when he walks in, will do it as he walks out," followed by the statement: "It's not that I'm racist," as if to validate the saying as fact, not based on racial prejudice. A man can be friends with a black person until he comes around to ask for the white daughter's hand in marriage. Most people are not bothered by an effeminate man and will even celebrate his wit and taste as long as he is not found sitting in the living room engaged in private chat with a son or brother. It's similar, as the comedian Tom Lehrer used to say, to a Christian Scientist with appendicitis.

Racism and homomisia find different ways of expressing themselves, sometimes unconsciously, because they are accepted realities of everyday life and no one notices the connotation as if culturally anesthetized. Otherwise, they can be explicitly offensive, intentionally hurtful. On certain occasions a *pato* is a gay gentleman who has just left the room, in Merle Miller's famous words. Similarly, in the last decades, when geographical relocation has been common, the non-white person can be Asian, Indian, African or Semitic just as well as they can be Muslim, Hindu, Buddhist, Christian or Jewish. Then racism can be tinged with xenophobia and religious bias, the fear of "the evil other." The other may not give reason at all to arouse suspesions of malfeasance: His or her mere existence makes him or her so.

Not as Black as They Seem

Dramatic art, despite its performance by the progressive and the enlightened, is not exempt from racism.

For example, the practice of applying black makeup on stage was known to be in use as far back as 1441 in Europe.[8] It was frequently used in Elizabethan and Jacobean theater, best known for William Shakespeare's *Othello, the Moor of Venice*. During the nineteenth century the practice spread throughout popular American theater and contributed to shaping an image of black people as caricatures, a being without worries or responsibility. The characters were dumb and foolish, coming from southern plantations, with exaggeratedly swollen lips, protruding eyes and tight-curl wigs. The genre was known as minstrel shows, a popular form of

---

[8] See John Strausbaugh, *Black Like You: Blackface, Whiteface, Insult and Imitation in American Popular Culture* (New York: Penguin, 2006), pp. 35-36.

entertainment, a stereotype that continued unchallenged until the 1960s.

Throughout the 1950s two of the best-known radio personalities (later also in film and TV) in the U.S. were Amos and Andy (*The Amos 'n Andy Show*). Neither actor was black; the characters were played by Alvin Childress and Spencer Williams, both white.[9] By the 60s black makeup to simulate African origins (*blackface*) alien to the performer's was considered to be mockery, a form of offensive racial impersonation that exploited and hyperbolically represented the physical features of a person to transform the represented as something grotesque. In the early 70s blackface disappeared from the artistic landscape on stage and on popular media in the U.S.; the United Kingdom had instances of the practice until 1981.

---

[9] Since the 1930s the character of Charlie Chan was well-known in American film. He was a very perceptive detective played by Wedish actor Warner Oland in Asian makeup. Oland played Asian roles in most of the movies he made between 1935 and 1948.

The blackface stereotype was an integral part of popular entertainment on radio and TV in pre-revolutionary Cuba. It persisted in outdated vaudeville performed by Cuban exiles in southern Florida. It was predominant in vulgar sketches fraught with tired plotlines and trite double entendre dialogue often involving sexual situations. The genre was still in place at least until the 90s.

It was customary to use black makeup on an actor to represent black roles on soap operas and variety shows in both Puerto Rico and Cuba during the 50s; while the Revolution removed the practice in popular media in Cuba, it did not end in Puerto Rico. As recently as 2010 a Cuban-exile program aired on Spanish-language TV in Miami, *Brown Sugar* (*Azúcar morena*), a made-for-TV film. It was based on a Cuban racist premise, with double-meant race-baiting dialogue. The performers were a talented Puerto Rican actress by the name of Lillian Hurst, who had played mostly bit parts on English-language film and TV, but was a well-known comedienne in Puerto Rico and Peru. Her character was a firm believer in white supremacy (Ms. Hurst is a blue-eyed blonde Puerto Rican). In the story her son, played by her real-life son Manolo Travieso, whose father Héctor is a Cuban soap-opera actor and TV political satire show host. This time the black character was played by a black woman, but subjected to the same stereotype. In the twenty-first century such a plotline is a clueless production of racial insensitivity. A show of that type on English-language TV in the U.S. would have caused an uproar of controversy and boycotts.

On American TV programs that broached racial themes from a similar perspective were replaced by programming compatible with social movements such as gay pride, feminism and black power: *Good Times*, *The Jeffersons*, *Sanford and Son*, for instance provided models and visions that diverged from traditional heteronormative, male-dominated contexts. The Latino culture was also presented from a different perspective in intercultural programs such as *Chico and the Man*. Popular entertainment included new images of the place of women in society, as were *The Mary Tyler Moore Show* , *One Day at a Time* and *Rhoda*, a precursor of which had been *Julia* (1968-71), whose lead character was a single mother, a professional black woman played by Dihann Carroll. Male domination became a caricature of bigotry in Norman Lear's *All in the Family* and *Maude*. Their plots exposed, denounced and ridiculed prejudice and self-inflicted ignorance.

The prototypical melodrama based on the themes of bourgeois honor and morality, options available to women and race relations in pre-revolutionary Cuba was *El derecho de nacer* (*The Right to be Born*), by Felix B. Caignet. The radio soap opera set audience records in the early 50s. This is the story of an aristocratic landowning family whose daughter falls in love with the wrong man, becomes pregnant and is banished from her home to a place in the mountains where she will deliver the baby, and her black nanny will dispose of the child. Upon the young woman's return to the urban setting she becomes a nun to atone for her sin. The black nanny raises the child as her own, claiming the boy's father was white. The boy grows up to become a famous doctor, Alberto Limonta, called upon to treat his unsuspecting grandfather, Don Rafael del Junco. The patient, an old and infirm man, decides to pay a visit to the doctor's home, where he is confronted with the truth as the nanny pounds him with hurtful words about his intention to get rid of the baby while the compassionate black woman disobeyed him and raised the child to be a decent and caring physician. Don Rafael immediately suffers a stroke. He cannot speak and thus cannot tell Alberto Limonta, his doctor and grandson, who he really is. His daughter, María Elena, now a nun, is called in to be by her father's side. Thanks to Dr. Limonta's treatment, eventually Don Rafael recovers his speech enough to reveal to both mother and son their true identities.

The radio soap was made into a film in 1953, a Cuban-Mexican production. Mexican actors Gloria Marín and José Baviera played two of the main roles, while the Spaniard Jorge Mistral was Albertico Limonta. The role of the black nanny, Mamá Dolores, was played by Lupe Suárez in blackface. This was in perfect consonance with the Cuban entertainment tradition: the only black characters on Cuban TV were white people in blackface. On the radio blacks were impersonated by whites who assumed the linguistic features of black people's speech in Cuba. Their utterances were staggered, final intervocalic *d* disappeared, and *s* in mid word and at the end were aspirated.

It was not until 1966 that a black woman played Mamá Dolores in a TV remake of the story, Eusebia Cosme, a Cuban exile. Later the character was reprised in a movie titled *Mamá Dolores* played by the same Eusebia Cosme. In Mexico she also appeared in film vehicles for the legendary Argentinian actress Libertad Lamarque, *El negro es un bello color* (*Black is a Beautiful Color*) and *Flores blancas para mi hermana negra* (*White Flowers for My Black Sister*).

Puerto Rico was not the exception to the practice. Since the beginnings of radio broadcasting in the island Ramón Rivero was the first non-black actor to play a black character, *Diplo*. When his show moved to WKAQ-TV as La taberna India (*The India Beer Tavern*) as a live sitcom, the character, black face and lips white and exaggeratedly swollen, became so popular that many in the general population knew the actor as Ramón Rivero Diplo.

The first movie made in Puerto Rico for international distribution by a local production company, *Maruja* (1959), featured Marta Romero and Mario Pabón (so pale he almost looked translucent). The plotline was a lurid tale about a woman who cheats on her husband with a powerful man in town, but when the man's son (Pabón) returns home after attending school abroad, Maruja turns her attention to the young man, himself engaged to his childhood girlfriend. A fellow barber in Maruja's husband shop is secretly in love with the woman. When he finds out she is having an affair with another man he kills her, then throws himself off a ferris wheel and dies during a town festival. Not a single black actor was included in the cast. Mona Marti played the role of someone'smother; she had also played the black nanny in the Puerto Rican TV version of *El derecho de nacer* the same way Lupe Suárez had in Cuba, in blackface.

Nonetheless, as in Cuba, where black musicians were extremely popular (for whites to listen and dance to, not to mingle with: Benny Moré, Rolando Lasserie, Celia Cruz) the only blacks in the film were mixed-race singer Ismael River and the Rafael Cortijo band, most of which consisted of black or mixed-race musicians. The band plays a song during a town festival in the film, "El negro bembón" ("The Fat-Lipped Negro"), whose composer was Puerto Rican Bobby Capó. The song was very popular at the time in the island. The lyrics refer to a police investigation of the murder of a black man. When the murderer is asked why he killed the other man, he says he killed him "for being such a fat-lipped nigger." The policeman then hides his own fat lips and says: "That's no reason to kill the fat-lipped man." The song's composer stated in interviews that it was supposed to be a humorous denunciation of a social nature.[10]

By that time the Cuban Revolution had stopped the practice, still common in the U.S. throughout the first half of the twentieth century of not allowing black performers to walk in through the main door of the venues where they appeared. Previously, however, in both Puerto Rico and Cuba non-white musicians would perform in whites-only clubs (in Puerto Rico the Escambrón and the Casino de Puerto Rico, where illegitimate offspring, regardless of race or social position, were not allowed

---

[10] In the Puerto Rican Theater Festival production of *La cuarterona* the role of Julia was played by Marta Romero, who also played the title role in *Maruja*, skin darkened for the stage.

membership; in Cuba, Centro Gallego and Club Deportivo) and hotel stages, but had to walk in through back doors, could not sit at the bar or become members regardless of their popularity, as Cuban singer Celia Cruz and Puerto Rican Ruth Fernandez often remembered during interviews.

The first black performer on Puerto Rican TV in the second half of the 50s was Carmen Belén Richardson, a gifted comedienne. Her role was of a girl with popping eyes and ringlets in white paper on her braided curly hair. Despite the pioneering element of her acting, she was given the name of *Lirio Blanco*, White Lily, obviously meant to mock her ancestry. Ms. Richardson gained popularity in the 70s as a black feminist in a Puerto Rican version of American TV's *Laugh-In*. Her name on that show was Concha Vienda, which read with the correct intonation was the equivalent of *con chavienda*: in Puerto Rican Spanish means "to upset and bother," as in "here it comes again to piss us off." The show's scriptwriters were all male.

The practice of using white actors to play black characters in blackface in the U.S. ended with the civil-rights movement and the acknowledgment of the rights of minorities at the end of the 60s. In Puerto Rico blackfaced illiterate characters continued to appear on TV in the 90s, with Angela Meyer's *Chianita.*, a foolish woman in curly hair and a white flower blossom stuck behind her ear. She recorded an album of songs composed with phrases with incorrect syntax and use of prepositions and object pronouns: "*Voten por yo*," for instance: "Vote for I," in a song promoting herself to be elected governor. She thus inserted herself in the outdated and offensive tradition that both the Cuban Revolution and the civil rights movement had erradicated from public media, for the benefit of an audience inoculated against racial sensitivity. During the 2016 electoral campaigns in Puerto Rico, Ms. Meyer resurrected her TV character of Chianita as a candidate for governor. Sadly for Ms. Meyer, the *deja vu* character had worn out its welcome and failed to attain the same impact it had in earlier times.

Blood Quantification in Literature

The term *quadroon* is applicable, historically, to a person of one-quarter black ancestry. Hegemonic classes used such terms for the purpose of specifying the legal and hereditary boundaries of a person and not only to indicate racial origin. While racial prejudice among whites toward blacks and among blacks themselves according to differences in skin darkness gradations and other distinctive racial features such as hair texture and nose and mouth shape, were useful for humiliating with the reminder of a perceived inferiority, it was also useful in official colonial matters. There were specific differences in inheritance claims for a mixed-raced heir even when recognized as natural issue of the deceased. The bias and inequality persist even to this day, albeit in subtle and less strident ways. The term *quadroon* has been replaced by *biracial* or *racially mixed* or *blended* when the need arises for specificity for sociological and demographic purposes. The words these have substituted are now considered archaic or in poor taste. The reference has changed, but the referent itself is oftentimes used with an intention as hurtful and humiliating as the older labels.[11]

In societies such as that of pre-revolutionary Cuba, for example, upper-class whites took pride in the fact that their country preserved racial purity. "Whites married whites, blacks married blacks, café au lait married café au lait, high yellow to high yellow. Crossing to the other side always brought bad consequences," explained to me a Cuban professor of sociology in a prestigious university in the U.S., whose father had been a prominent Jewish Cuban geographer before the Revolution. A Cuban professor in a well-known

---

[11] See Conrad P. Kottaki, *Mirror for Humanity: A Concise Introduction to Cultural Ahthropology* (New York: MacGraw-Hill, 2009), chap. 11, Ethnicity and Race.

northeastern university expressed a similar concept to me around 1980: the man held doctoral degrees in education and law from the University of Havana in the mid-50s. In Havana he had been a deputy minister of education and a founding member of an exclusive professional society of José Martí scholars. "When a white man married a black woman he ruined his race," he told me during a lunch break. Something similar happened in the American South, specially in societies whose economy was based on sugar-cane production, such as Louisiana, the Mississippi delta and Florida.

Even when the opposite is affirmed for reasons of national and critical enthusiasm among Puerto Rican scholars, Alejandro Tapia y Rivera's work did not spring from a literary vacuum. He was not the first to approach the theme of interracial relations in Latin America nor the first to explore the abolitionist subject in Spanish-language literature. In Cuba Cirilo Veillaverde did so in *Cecilia Valdés o la Loma del Ángel* (*Cecilia Valdes or the Angel's Hill*) in 1839; Villaverde had also published a minor work titled *The Slave Hunter*, that dealt with the inhumanity of the slave trade and the people who worked for slave owners in Cuba. The *Cecilia Valdés...* novel was widely read in the Spanish-speaking world much earlier than *The Quadroon* was even written, certainly before the play opened in 1878, provoking lukewarm critical and public reactions.

The literary representation of abuse and injustice in the social categorization of blacks in Latin America was *The Autobiography of a Slave* (1835), by Cuban writer Juan Francisco Manzano. In 1841, 26 years before *La cuarterona* was published in Madrid, Gertrudis Gómez de Avellaneda, also from Cuba, published her abolitionist novel *Sab*.[12]

Antislavery writers in the U.S. used a character of mixed race, real and fictional, to win over the good will and support of

---

[12] See Nydia Jeffers, "El protagonista negro en la narrativa antiesclavista latinoamericana del siglo XIX". Ph.D. dissertation. University of Nebraska-Lincoln, 2009.

Americans in abolitionist efforts. The figure of a man of deeply dark skin was potentially unpleasant and offensive. Lighter-skinned people, however, stimulated stronger feelings of humanity and compassion—abolitionists used that feality to recruit followers and like-minded allies before the American Civil War.[13]

In American literature James Fennimore Cooper brings up the subject of bias against quadroons in his character of Cora in his 1826 novel, *The Last of the Mohicans*. That same year Henry Wadsworth Lonfellow wrote the poem "The Quadroon Girl," the narration of the tragedy of a young girl when a wealthy landowner sells his quadroon daughter to a slave who desired her for sexual satisfaction. In *Song of Myself* (1855) Walt Whitman includes a poem about an auctioned quadroon girl.

Between 1836 and 1865 the character of the tragic mulatto was common in

---

[13] See Richard Jackson, *The Black Image in Latin American Literature* (Albuquerque, New Mexico: University of New Mexico Press, 1976).

American literature. The first known of such stock characters was Archy Moore, the main character in a novel titled *The White Slave or Memories of a Fugitive*, by Richard Hildreth. A short story in American abolitionist literature from 1851, of extensive distribution, was *The Quadroons*, by Lydia Maria Child[14]: Xanta is the daughter of Edward, a white man from Georgia, and a quadroon, Rosalie. Xanta ignores her racial origin before being victimized by the slavery system. When it becomes known that Rosalie's grandmother was a runaway slave, Xanta loses her freedom and comfortable life to become a slave.

As a female character in abolitionist literature the quadroon is usually raised in her biological father's home and passes for white. The family's financial ruin makes

---

[14] Lydia Maria Child (1802-1880) was an abolitionist feminist, considered the first white woman who openly struggled for the rights of slaves. She had written about the subject in her 1833 book *An Appeal in Favor of That Class of Americans called Africans.*

.

the quadroon a victim of moral misery, a literary stock mechanism that abolitionist writers used to convey the notion of the sexual exploitation to which slave masters subjected non-white women. A typical literary work in that genre was *The Quadroon or Adventures of a Lover in Louisiana* (1856), by Thomas Mayne Reid (also writer of the more popular *The Headless Horseman*). Reid turned the novel into a successful stage play in 1859, produced at the Winter Garden Theater in New York under the title of *The Octoroon*.

In post-bellum South literary works broached the subject of the descendancy of Africans in a different way. The goal was no longer abolitionist, but to present the penury of former slaves and their progeny, as well as the persistence of prejudice despite the official change in social status. The exception was Thomas Dixon's novel *The Clansman: A Historical Romance of the Ku Klux Klan* (1905). The novel was a glorification of the racist organization also known as the Invisible Empire of the

South, which began in the South after the Civil War, but had also spread to northern states by the turn of the century. D. W. Griffith made it a movie, *Birth of a Nation*. One of the first private screenings of the film was in 1915 in the White House for then president Woodrow Wilson, a native Virginian whose childhood home is a state historical monument in Columbia, South Carolina.

The Awakening and *Desireé's Baby*, by Kate Chopin, are examples of the new perspective. However, it would not be until the Harlem Renaissance during the first third of the twentieth century that black and blended-race writers began publishing their writing from their own viewpoint. They recorded their memories, projects, dreams and lives crushed by racial inequality. However, as the century progressed those writers became the conscience of a people still victimized, but rising and rebelling against oppression.

Tapia y Rivera's Reaction to the Avoidance of the Topic of Racism

If the character of the mulatto or quadroon or any other category ranked according to fractions of blood purity is not new in literature and not even in Tapia y Rivera's time when he wrote *La cuarterona*, what exactly is the basis for his literary importance or the cultural impact of his work? In a way that question is equivalent to asking: if the central character in chivalry novels already existed, what did Cervantes' *Don Quixote* add to the genre? We can consider two reasons for Tapia y Rivera's place in Spanish-language literature.

First: The subject and the perspective, which Tapia y Rivera approached before anyone else in Puerto Rican literature did. The writer was a pioneer in looking at the matter of racial prejudice with a focus on an individual, but with social repercussions. It is of primordial importance to keep this in the forefront of any discussion of the stage play because no one else since then has so deeply delved into the subject in Puerto Rican literature until late in the twentieth century. Even this resurgence of the racial issue took place incidentally, as in Luis Rafael Sánchez in *Macho Camacho's Beat*.

The black theme has been brought up in literature after Tapia y Rivera mostly from the standpoint of tropicalism and the exotic. This is particularly true of the *negroide* poetry of Luis Palés Matos. "Black Majesty," his best-known work of an Afro-Antillean content, is an apostrophic celebration of every frivolously sultry stereotype of mixed-race females, reminiscent of the roles Puerto Rican actress Rita Moreno played early in her film career (as Rosa Zacharias in the screen version of Tennessee Williams' *Summer and Smoke*, for example, when she was known as "Rita the Cheetah). It reminds the informed reader of all the unfortunate qualities ascribed to the *mulato* in Cuba while slavery was legal: carefree, seductive and lascivious. The poem's beat is decidedly erotic, as poetry performer Juan Boria discovered as he adopted his interpretation of "Black Majesty" as his hallmark act: his delivery was full of suggestive gestures and hip gyrations. In African-sounding onomatopoeic, alliterative words that may be meaningless (*tembandumba*, *cumbamba*, *cumba macumba*, *candombe*, *bomba que bamba*) the poet calls a voluptuous black woman "Flower of Tortola, Rose of Uganda," then proceeds to describe her walking rhythm: "Shaking her ass the queen advances, and from her immense croup slip arousing shakes that the Congo gels in rivers of sugar and syrup, black sugar mill of sensuous harvest..." "Ñam-ñam" ("Yum-yum") is another of Palés Matos' poems that exploits prejudice and myths about Africans, in this case anthropophagy: "Black teeth on white flesh..."

Aside from *La cuarterona*, no twentieth century Puerto Rican playwright has even included the subject of racial prejudice and social inequality based on non-white ancestry. Predominant themes in twentieth and twenty-first-century drama in Puerto Rico are bourgeois concerns regarding politics and individual alienation in both Puerto Rico and the American metropolis. Most notable of the writers who avoid the racial subject is the novelist and playwright Luis Rafael Sánchez, himself of blended-race ancestry. Sánchez focuses on the feminine psyche and Judeo-Christian and classical European mythology and Puerto Rico's nexus to them: *The Passion According to Antigone Pérez, The Angels Have Fatigued, Our Daily Gall.*, the stories collected in *In Shirt Sleeves*, for example. The characters are females marginalized by political forces, sexual exploitation and misogyny. No Puerto Rican female writer is as feminist as Sánchez.

There are two exceptions to the lack of coverage of racial bias in Puerto Rican theater. Withthis play, *The 'Plena' Died in Maragüez* (1977), Juan González touched on the subject or race, but only insofar as the lead character, Isabel La Negra, was of African ancestry. Based on a real-life influential brothel owner in southern Puerto Rico, however, the racial aspect was almost incidental as the work focuses on local politics and the powerful who reached significant decisions and made political agreements while patronizing the infamous whorehouse.[15] . More to the point, Roberto Ramos Perea's 2018 play, *Por maricón* (*Because You Are a Fag*), addresses both homophobia and racism in Puerto Rico during the nineteenth century.

A few years ago a Puerto Rican literature scholar claimed during a radio broadcast that *La cuarterona* was more valuable as a stage play than a novel such as Cirilo Villaverde's *Cecilia Valdés or the Angel's Hill*, which preceded Tapia y Rivera's drama. "Half a dozen people read a novel," he affirmed, "but a play is seen by thousands of people." Without attempting to take any achievements away from the self-described *tapiano*, his assertion is perplexing. It is neither fair nor appropriate to compare the two works. Furthermore, it is

---

[15] *La plena murió* en Maragüez is an exploración de intersection of politics, influence, power and sexuality in Puerto Rico during the twentieth century. Its debut was at the Humacao campus of the University of Puerto Rico in 1978 with the academic sponsorship of Dr. Juan Antonio Rodríguez Pagán. TV actress Lucy Boscana played the role of Isabel la Negra. A critic in the theater that night whispered in my ear that he could not understand why Boscana thought she needed blackface.

not a valid argument with which to defend one work against the other, particularly when the intention is to present a literary work as inferior to another on the basis of (falsely claimed) access or attraction. As dramatic characters Julia and Cecilia share only a racial origin. Villaverde wrote a cautionary tale with a moral message from a classic Romantic perspective, high above the poor devils down below. *Cecilia Valdés...* is the type of novel the Spaniard Mariano José de Larra would have written if he had been a novelist instead of a journalist and acerbic social critic who zeroed in on the customs of the lower classes and the bourgeoisie. Tapia y Rivera denounces social injustice.

Cecilia Valdés is a caricature of the literary stereotype of the *mulata* created by Cuban society.[16] She is neither tragic nor suffering, although she comes to a tragic end. She is completely without scruples. Her motivation for marrying a white man is to become a member of the upper class and

---

[16] See Cileine de Lourenço. "Representación racial y ambigüedad en la narrativa fundacional." *Revista Iberoamericana*, 68:199, April-June 2002: 317-330.

share in the white world. She's voluptuous, fiery, impudent, vital, manipulative. She drives Leonardo to the despair of desire; he calls her irresistible. Leonardo is married to Luisa, a daughter of privilege, a white judgmental woman and a member of the hegemonic spheres, but he lusts after Cecilia, the sensuous, flirtatious *mulata*, who, in turn, is aware of her charms and uses them to her advantage.[17]

La cuarterona's Carlos calls Julia his idol, his goddess, the object of his adoration and veneration. Cecilia would not have fixed her eyes on him or on his hedonist friend Luis, because, although of differing genders, Cecilia and Luis are two sides of the same opportunistic moral coin.

Cecilia's tragedy is that she is obsessed capriciously with Leonardo without knowing he is her brother, children of the same

---

[17] See Sara V. Rosell, "Cecilia Valdés de Villaverde a Arenas: La (re)creación del mito de la mulata." *Afro-Hispanic Review* 18:2 (1999): 15-21; Zoila Clark, "El cristianismo y los estereotipos de la mujer en la novelas cubanas de la esclavitud: *Francisco: al ingenio o las delicias del campo, Cecilia Valdés* y *Sab.*" *Sin Frontera: Revista Académica y Literaria*, 1.1 (2006).

father, Cándido de Gamboa. Julia's is that she is iin love with the son of hegemonic nobility, engaged to Julia's sister Emilia, neither of whom know of their shared origin. That fact is revealed to everyone in the play and to the public during the last minutes. While incest is Cecilia's sin, it is only the lie the *Condesa* fabricates to mislead Carlos and separate him from the illegitimate daughter of his fiancé's father: the *Condesa* herself does not know who Julia's father was. Carlos is to forego his love for Julia to make it possible for him to marry Emilia for the sake of his mother's fear of financial ruin and Emilia's arriviste father.

Second, the greatness of *La cuarterona*, and more important yet, is founded on Tapia y Rivera's technique as a dramatist. The structure of the play is flawless in its Romantic respect for the classic unities of time, place and action. Conflicts are revealed in a relentless crescendo of intensity. The play affords the audience no emotional respite. Only the character of Luis brings a certain measure of comic relief, but his humor is of such a cynical nature that it leads to a feeling close to nausea. Tapia y Rivera hammers constantly on the conflict, gives us a grain of hope that something could happen in favor of Julia and Carlos' romance, but no,, we are immediately denied any solution other than what is proposed by the controlling interests and, within the dramatic and emotional space Tapia y Rivera builds, literary immorality.

In the play's focus on the dilemmas of each character (other than Carlos and Julia), whose duplicity of motives is presented in opportune and revealing asides, we cannot see the individual knots as limited to individuals. They are instead representative of an entire class of people. Don Críspulo is the social climber who, it is suggested, considering that since 1820 the slave trade was prohibited in Spanish colonies, is involved in slave smuggling as he refers to obstacles in his commercial enterprise dealing with *negritos*, darkies. Don Críspulo also stands for the feudal white slave trader who rapes without consideration of the consequences of his incontinence and from his conviction that it is his right. *La Condesa*, whose north is her class consciousness and dignity intimately tied to wealth is willing to sacrifice her own son when necessary to keep her place in a social context that mirrors her shallowness. Additionally her character represents the effects of the economic system that caused an international financial crisis in 1847. Although it is not mentioned in the play, the writer may have taken for granted the audience's response to the *Condesa*'s situation, as many fortunes in Cuba crashed under the circumstances and drove many formerly wealthy people to destitution.

Emilia is an unfortunate result of the social and economic environment that sustains her. Luis, on the other hand, hangs around like a vulture and befriends Emilia with nefarious intentions in the event that his friend Carlos does not marry her, is a superficial opportunist, a selfish and parasitic member of the creole bourgeoisie who aspires to the human barrel-bottom of social heights. He would consider marriage as a form of legalized procurement under the guise of marriage to someone like Emilia, while also lusting after innocent and clueless Julia.

Julia is doubly victimized, on one side by the *Condesa* and her merciless demands of her renunciation to Carlos, and, on the other, by her awareness of her debt of gratitude and loyalty to the *Condesa* as an inferior woman unworthy of happiness.

Finally, Carlos is perhaps the most tragic representative of pure idealism, the social element that attempts to tear through the thick tapestry that keeps him from reaching his goal of defeating a prejudice as socially pernicious as it is alien to his kindness. He strives for a noble bliss that eludes him at every step, from the play's start to its end.

It is difficult to imagine a more simultaneously tender and bitter moment in Puerto Rican or even Spanish-language literature in general than the dialogues between Carlos and Julia and the ones in the third act of *La cuarterona*. In this last act Carlos begs his mother to listen to him, to give him his blessing for his union with Julia. He promises the financially-strapped *Condesa* that he will provide for her and keep her through his medical profession, deluded in his belief that only the economic issue stands in the way of her approval of his marriage to Julia. This thus evinces, without any need for Tapia y Rivera to make it obvious with additional lines, that it is the *Condesa*'s conscience of class and social status that prevents her from consenting.

As a reader, literary critic and playwright, I have only found a similar scene in Spanish literature that has so deeply moved me the same way as the exchanges between Carlos in his anguish and frustration with his mother's obstinate attitude. When El Cid, Ruy Díaz de Vivar, in the *Poem of Mio Cid* is about to leave behind his wife Jimena and his young daughters Doña Elvira and Doña Sol while he goes off to do battle to earn a living. The minstrel's simile to describe the moment is: "As the finger nail torn from the flesh is his pain," to succinctly poiont to the emotional state of the departing husband and father. The emotional load of the scene between the *Condesa* and Carlos strips the shell off classist injustice and racial prejudice to reveal the deep scars of their consequences. Tapia y Rivera thus demonstrates that tenderness and reason are not antithetic, that they can inhabit together the human soul, that the inevitability of the destruction of one life to raise another is false, specially when goals are noble and merciful rather than intrinsically vile.

Trascendence and permanence

La cuarterona first opened in San Juan in 1878 with neither the critic nor box office success the author and producers expected. Perhaps it is necessary to consider the sociology of live theater regarding audiences to find an explanation: it certainly was not the lack of scriptwriting artistry.

Slavery in Puerto Rico had been abolished five years earlier. The play was written during an abolitionist trend, but opened under an antiracist banner.

For what public does the curtain come up, mostly? Who had the means to buy theater tickets at that specific moment in time? Certainly not freed slaves, perhaps abolitionist stragglers, but the majority of the public who could take the time and afford the price of a ticket were predominantly the class that lost chattel when slavery was abolished, the same people Tapia y Rivera confronted, upfront and viscerally. The play picked on the yet to be scabbed ulcer of that about which the Puerto Rican theater-going public wanted to address or discuss.

However, time has been much more favorable to Tapia y Rivera. What was short in public perception then, the public that could not recognize the worth of the work, has been abundant in subsequent generations—fortunately.

A Minimal Bibliography on
Alejandro Tapia y Rivera

Printed

Acevedo de Quintana, Camelia. "La mujer en la obra de Alejandro Tapia y Rivera". Tesis de maestría. Universidad de Puerto Rico (Recinto de Río Piedras), 1981.

Acevedo Marrero, Ramón Luis. "Los límites de la narrativa indianista en Puerto Rico: Tapia, Betances y Marqués". *Revista de Estudios Hispánicos* (Universidad de Puerto Rico) 25.1-2 (1998): 93-111.

___. "Alejandro Tapia y René Marqués: Los límites de la narrativa indigenista en Puerto Rico". *Actas del congreso Alejandro Tapia y Rivera*. Ed. Rubén Alejandro Moreira. San Juan, Puerto Rico: Ateneo Puertorriqueño, 2004. 105-120.

Álvarez Curbelo, Silvia. "El olor de la azucena: La feminización en la escritura de Alejandro Tapia". *Actas del congreso Alejandro Tapia y Rivera*. Ed. Rubén Alejandro Moreira. San Juan, Puerto Rico: Ateneo Puertorriqueño, 2004. 7-15.

Aponte Alsina, Marta. *Póstumo interrogado: relectura de Tapia". Tapia ayer y hoy. Edición conmemorativa 1882-1982*. Ed. Marta Aponte y otros. Santurce: Universidad del Sagrado Corazón, 1982. 43-69.

- - -. "Tapia y Rivera, Alejandro". *Diccionario enciclopédico de las letras de América Latina vol.3*. Caracas: Biblioteca Ayacucho y Monte Ávila Editores Latinoamericana. 1995: 4630- 4632.

Aponte Ramos, Lola. "Geografía discursiva del límite del color: Los textos de Alejandro Tapia y Rivera ante la raza". *Actas del congreso de Alejandro Tapia y Rivera*. Ed. Rubén Alejandro Moreira. San Juan, Puerto Rico: Ateneo Puertorriqueño, 2004. 77-86.

Arrillaga, María. "La mujer en *La Sataniada* de Alejandro Tapia y Rivera". *Actas del congreso Alejandro Tapia y Rivera*. Ed. Rubén

Alejandro Moreira. San Juan, Puerto Rico: Ateneo Puertorriqueño, 2004. 19-36.

Beauchamp, José Juan. *Imagen del puertorriqueño en la novela (en Alejandro Tapia y Rivera, Manuel Zeno Gandía y Enrique A. Laguerre)*. Río Piedras, P.R.: Editorial Universitaria, Universidad de Puerto Rico, 1976.

Bernabé Riefkohl, Rafael. "Género y frontera: *Póstumo el transmigrado* de Alejandro Tapia". *Revista de Estudios Hispánicos* (Universidad de Puerto Rico) 20 (1993): 233-51.

Burgos, Lena. "Algunas ideas para una posible lectura de la construcción del sujeto moderno en *Póstumo el transmigrado*". Actas del congreso Alejandro Tapia y Rivera. Ed. Rubén Alejandro Moreira. San Juan, Puerto Rico: *Ateneo Puertorriqueño*, 2004. 143-150.

Carretero, Manuel. "Martí, Tapia y Rizal....olvidados de ultramar". *El Vocero* July 11, 1988, San Juan, P.R.: E22-E23.

Castro Pérez, Elsa. *Tapia: señalador de caminos*. San Juan, P.R.: Editorial Coquí, 1964.

Colón, Emilio M. (Ed.) *Alejandro Tapia y Rivera su vida y su obra*. Río Piedras, Puerto Rico: Editorial Coquí, 1971.

Córdova Iturregui, Félix. "A propósito de Alejandro Tapia: la ciudad ausente o las visiones de un cegato". *Revista de Estudios Hispánicos* (Universidad de Puerto Rico) 29.1-2 (2002): 25- 32.

___. "A Alejandro Tapia". *Milenio* 4.1 (2000): 251-252.

Dávila, Arturo. "Tapia todo un siglo". *El Nuevo Día* July 181982, San Juan, P.R.: 10.

Díaz, Luis Felipe. "El discurso liberal de Tapia y Rivera, Hostos y Zeno Gandía". *La na(rra)ción en la literatura puertorriqueña*. San Juan, P.R. : Ediciones Huracán, 2008. 54-80.

___. "Ironía e ideología en el discurso del siglo XIX: Alonso, Tapia y Rivera, Hostos y Zeno Gandía". *Revista de Estudios Hispánicos* (Univsidad de Puerto Rico) 29.1-2 (2002): 49-69.

Echevarría, Mónica. "Emblema de una era romántica". *El Nuevo Día* February 22, 2009, San Juan, P.R.: 42.

Fernández Valledor, Roberto. "Censura, censores y *La Sataniada*". *Revista del Centro de Estudios Avanzados de Puerto Rico* 18 (1994): 69-76.

___. "Ideología y recursos novelescos en *Póstumo el transmigrado* de Tapia". *Revista del Instituto de Cultura Puertorriqueño* 3.6 (2002): 19-30.

___. "Tapia en sus memorias". *Focus* 7.1 (2008) 73-80.

Ferrar, Heriberto. "*Bernardo de Palissy*". *Claridad* April 2-8, 1993, San Juan, P.R.: 26.

García Díaz, Manuel. *Alejandro Tapia y Rivera: su vida y su obra*. San Juan, PR: Editorial Coquí, 1964.

García Moll, Solange. "Notas para el diseño de *La Cuarterona*: La "ínsula desgraciada" en el teatro de Alejandro Tapia y Rivera". *Actas del congreso Alejandro Tapia y Rivera*. Ed. Rubén Alejandro Moreira. San Juan, Puerto Rico: Ateneo Puertorriqueño, 2004. 67-76.

Gómez Tejera, Carmen. "Alejandro Tapia y Rivera". *American Literature* 4.1 (1930): 20-23.

González, Leyra E. "¡Que empiece la función!". *El Nuevo Día* 20 de mayo de 2008, San Juan, P.R.: 76.

González Pérez, Aníbal. "La cuarterona and Slave Society in Cuba and Puerto Rico". *Latin American Literary Review* 8.15 (1980): 47-54.

Luiña de Palés, Angélica. "De Alejandro Tapia y Rivera: *La leyenda de los veinte años*". *El Mundo* February 24, 1962, San Juan, P.R.: 30.

Manrique Cabrera, Francisco. *Historia de la literatura puertorriqueña.* Río Piedras, P.R.: Editorial Cultural. 1977: 114-126 .

Martín Montes, José Luis. *Alejandro Tapia y su poema La Sataniada.* Río Piedras, P.R. : Universidad de Puerto Rico, 1957.

_ _ _. "Alejandro Tapia y su poema "La Sataniada". *Asomante* 12.2 (1956): 78- 94. Martínez

Capó, Juan. "Alejandro Tapia". *El Mundo* February 6, 1983, San Juan, P.R.: 7.

Martínez Solá, Jorge. "Bernardo de Palissy Changes Attitudes". *The San Juan Star* March 10, 1993, San Juan, P.R.: 10.

Meléndez, Concha. "Alejandro Tapia y Rivera". *Asomante* 1.1 (1945): 56-57.

Morfi, Angelina. *Historia crítica de un siglo de teatro puertorriqueño.* San Juan, P.R.: Instituto de Cultura Puertorriqueña, 1980.

Morán, Lucas. "El costumbrista Alejandro Tapia". *El Nuevo Día* November 11, 1984, San Juan, P.R.: 17-19.

Moreira, Rubén Alejandro. "*La Sataniada*: Ironía cósmica en el romanticismo puertorriqueño". *Actas del congreso Alejandro Tapia y Rivera.* Ed. Rubén Alejandro Moreira. San Juan, Puerto Rico: Ateneo Puertorriqueño, 2004. 37-46.

Pasarell, Emilio J. *Orígenes y desarrollo de la afición teatral en Puerto Rico*, Tomo 2. San Juan, P.R.: Editorial Universitaria, 1967.

___. *Panorama teatral de Puerto Rico en el siglo XIX.* San Juan, P.R.: Instituto de Cultura

Puertorriqueña, 1960.

Pérez Rivera, Tatiana. "El primer puertorriqueño". *El Nuevo Día* 11 de diciembre de 2008, San Juan, P.R.: 87.

_ _ _ . "De Tapia la primera carpeta". *El Nuevo Día* 20 de mayo de 2008, San Juan, P.R.: 52- 53.

Ramos Escobar, José Luis. "Tapia ayer y hoy". *Claridad* 8 al 14 de abril de 1983, San Juan, P.R.: (suplemento En Rojo).

Ramos Perea, Roberto. "El dramaturgo puertorriqueño Alejandro Tapia y Rivera ante los dramaturgos puertorriqueños de su tiempo". *Exégesis: Revista del Colegio Universitario de Humacao – UPR* 12.36 (2000): 40-47.

Rauch, Karen L. "Cuba on My Mind: The Role of the Sister Island in Alejandro Tapia y Rivera's Nationalist Literary Project". Middle Atlantic Council of Latin American Studies: *Latin American Essays* 19 (2006): 149-58.

Rivera, Ángel A. *Alejandro Tapia y Rivera y Eugenio María de Hostos: Avatares de una modernidad caribeña.* New York, NY: Peter Lang, WPI Studies 21, 2001.

- - -. "De fronteras, transexuales, y supervivencia: Dos casos en la literatura puertorriqueña, siglos XIX y XX". *Revista del Ateneo puertorriqueño* 5.13-15 (1995): 94-118.

_ _ _. "*Póstumo el transmigrado* o el tormento de los cuerpos". *Actas del congreso Alejandro Tapia y Rivera.* Ed. Rubén Alejandro Moreira. San Juan, Puerto Rico: Ateneo Puertorriqueño, 2004. 151-160.

_ _ _. "Puerto Rico on the Borders: Cultures of Survival or the Survival of Culture". *Latin American Literary* Review 26.51 (1998): 31-46.

_ _ _. "Siglo XIX, Alejandro Tapia y Rivera y *Mis memorias*: tecnologías del martirio y la configuración del yo". *Revista de Estudios Hispánicos* (Universidad de Puerto Rico) 23 (1996): 275-294.

Rivera de Álvarez, Josefina. *Literatura puertorriqueña. Su proceso en el tiempo.* Madrid: Partenón. 1983: 143-151.

Rivera Villegas, Carmen M. "Convergencias coloniales en dos autobiografías puertorr iqueñas". *Revista Interamericana* 25.1 (1995): 106-115.

Rodríguez, Jorge. "*La cuarterona* un examen del prejuicio racial". *El Vocero* March 17, 2000,, San Juan, P.R.: E4-E5.

Rodríguez González, Jose Luis. "Puerto Rico en *Mis memorias* de Alejandro Tapia y Ri-vera". M.A. thesis. Centro de Estudios Avanzados de Puerto Rico y el Caribe, 1987.

Rojas Osorio, Carlos. "El hegelianismo de las *Con-ferencias de estética y literatura*". *Actas del congreso Alejandro Tapia y Rivera*. Ed. Ru-bén Alejandro Moreira. San Juan, Puerto Rico: Ateneo Puertorriqueño, 2004. 121-130.

Román Eyxarch, Jazmina. "*Póstumo el transmi-grado* y *Póstumo el envirginado*". *Actas del congreso Alejandro Tapia y Rivera*. Ed. Ru-bén Alejandro Moreira. San Juan, Puerto Rico: Ateneo Puertorriqueño, 2004. 131-142.

___. "La estética de las novelas de Alejandro Tapia y Rivera en la formación de una etnia puertorriqueña". Ph.D. dissertation. Temple University, 1991.

Sáez, Antonia. *El teatro en Puerto Rico (Notas para su historia)*. Río Piedras: Editorial Universitaria, 1950.

Serrano de Matos, Magdalena. "El teatro de Alejandro Tapia y Rivera". Tesis de maestría. Universidad de Puerto Rico (Recinto de Río Piedras), 1953.

Solá, María E. y Elsa Arroyo. *"La cuarterona* de Alejandro Tapia: ¿Se parece a una novela de televisión?". *Revista del Ateneo Puertorriqueño* 3.8 (1993): 204-11.

Stevens, Camilla. "Ponernos el espejo por delante: Staging Race in Alejandro Tapia y Rivera's *La cuarterona". Revista Canadiense de Estudios Hispánicos* 31.2 (2007): 231-52.

Torres Pou, Joan. "Memorias de Puerto Rico: la historia en la prosa de Alejandro Tapia y Rivera". *Hispamérica* 23.67 (1994): 33-41.

Trelles, Carmen D. "Tapia defensor de las mujeres". *El Nuevo Día* 27 de marzo de 1983, San Juan, P.R.: 10.

Electronic Media

http://bibliotecavirtualut.suagm.edu/biblioteca%20y%20persona%20del%20mes/Personajedelmes/ATR/ATR.htm

https://www.youtube.com/watch?v=JrKuQmelvBU. Entrevista con el dramaturgo puertorriqueño Roberto Ramos Perea, 3 de mayo del 2014 por Voz del Centro (vozdelcentro.org), sobre Alejandro Tapia y Rivera.

Most Significant Works by Tapia y Rivera

El heliotropo, 1848.
La palma del cacique, 1852.
Guarionex, ópera con estreno en 1854.
José Campeche, biografía, 1854.
Roberto D'Evreux, 1856.
Bernardo de Palyssy o el heroísmo del trabajo,
        1857.
La antigua sirena, 1862.

La cuarterona, 1867
Camoens, 1868.
Póstumo el transmigrado, 1872.
Vasco Núñez de Balboa, biografía, 1872.
Ramón Power, biografía, 1873.
La leyenda de los veinte años, 1874.
La sataniada, 1874.
Roberto Cofresí, 1876.
La parte del león, 1880.
Misceláneas, 1880.
Póstumo el envirginado, 1882.
Mis memorias; unfinished, published
     posthumously in 1927.

About the Author

 Joseph F. Delgado (José Delgado Figueroa) is the author of the only dual-language annotated edition of Alejandro Tapia y Rivera's *La cuarterona*. He received a Ph.D. in and linguistics and speech communication from the University of Minnesota and a law degree from the University of Pittsburgh. He has been a literary critic for *Publishers Weekly*'s Spanish edition and taught linguistics at the universities of Minnesota, Puerto Rico and South Carolina; at Carnegie Mellon University he was a researcher in linguistics applied to robotics. Delgado is the author of *The Rhetoric of Change: Metaphor and Politics in the Commonwealth of Puerto Rico* and award-winning plays in the U.S., as well as short-story collections and novels such as *Our Father Takes a Bride*. Among his independent film work are *Luigi Pirandello's Six Characters in Search of an Author* and *The Friar's Lantern*. He is a PEN Club member and makes South Carolina his home.

Made in United States
Orlando, FL
30 December 2024